DATE DUE

DEMCO 138298

CELEBRATE HOLIDAYS

Celebrate Kwanzaa

Linda Jacobs Altman

This family lights a kinara for Kwanzaa.

Enslow Publishers, Inc.
40 Industrial Road
Box 398
Berkeley Heights, NJ 07922
USA

http://www.enslow.com

Library of Congress Cataloging-in-Publication Data

Altman, Linda Jacobs, 1943–
    Celebrate Kwanzaa / Linda Jacobs Altman.
    p. cm. — (Celebrate holidays)
  Includes bibliographical references and index.
  ISBN-13: 978-0-7660-2862-3
  ISBN-10: 0-7660-2862-3
  1. Kwanzaa—Juvenile literature. I. Title.
  GT4403.A47 2008
  394.2612—dc22
                2006034031

Printed in the United States of America

10 9 8 7 6 5 4 3 2 1

To Our Readers:
We have done our best to make sure all Internet Addresses in this book were active and appropriate when we went to press. However, the author and the publisher have no control over and assume no liability for the material available on those Internet sites or on other Web sites they may link to. Any comments or suggestions can be sent by e-mail to comments@enslow.com or to the address on the back cover.

Every effort has been made to locate all copyright holders of material used in this book. If any errors or omissions have occurred, corrections will be made in future editions of this book.

Illustration Credits: © 1999 Artville, LLC., p. 90; Associated Press, pp. 10, 18, 30, 32, 43, 47, 50, 64, 76, 78, 80; Black Star / Alamy, p. 56; The British Library / Topham-HIP / The Image Works, p. 15; Department of Special Collections, Charles E. Young Research Library, UCLA, pp. 24, 29; Colette Fournier / The Image Works, p. 68; The Granger Collection, p. 7; iStockphoto.com / Terry White, p. 87; © 2007 Jupiterimages, pp. 5, 19, 33, 51, 54, 57, 58, 65, 77, 89 (all); Library of Congress, pp. 21, 39; Mary Evans Picture Library / The Image Works, p. 12; Lawrence Migdale / Photo Researchers, Inc., p. 71; Shuterstock, pp. 2-3 (background), 4, 5 (background), 9, 13, 19 (background), 33 (background), 46 (background), 51 (background), 55, 59 (background), 60, 62 (background), 65 (background), 66 (background), 77 (background), 82-83 (background), 89 (background); (c) Corbis/Punchstock, p. 1; Time & Life Pictures / Getty Images, p. 35.

Cover Illustration: © Corbis/Punchstock

CONTENTS

◆ Chapter 1. **Harvest Festivals Around the World** **5**

◆ Chapter 2. **The Life of Maulana Karenga** . . . **19**

◆ Chapter 3. **Kwanzaa and African-American Culture** **33**

◆ Chapter 4. **Symbols, Rituals, and Traditions** **51**

◆ Chapter 5. **The Principles of Kwanzaa** **65**

◆ Chapter 6. **Celebrating Kwanzaa Today** **77**

Not-So-Famous Tribute Poem **89**

Glossary **91**

Chapter Notes **93**

Further Reading **99**

Internet Addresses **101**

Index **102**

Harvest Festivals Around the World

The holiday of Kwanzaa is a mystery to some people. It uses African ideas, but it is not African. It is African-American. It uses time-honored symbols, but it is not ancient. It was created in 1966.

Founder Maulana Karenga gave the new holiday a feeling of long tradition. He did this by basing Kwanzaa on one of the oldest celebrations in human history: the harvest festival.

Harvest festivals grew out of the agricultural revolution, which started about ten thousand years ago. Until then, people lived in small bands, building their lives around the never ending search for food. Farming let them settle down and build stable communities.

Festivals soon followed. Though different cultures have different customs, their purpose is the same: to celebrate the harvest and give thanks for it.

Whole communities come together to create a special time for all to share. In some traditions, attendance is a religious or cultural duty. For example, Jews were required to gather at the Temple in Jerusalem for the harvest festival of Succoth.

Succoth: The Jewish Festival of Booths

Succoth, or booths, were the temporary shelters the Hebrews used during their wanderings in the wilderness. According to tradition, a succah (singular of succoth) should not be built to last. Its walls should be flimsy, its roof made of thatch. There should be gaps in the roof so people can see the stars from inside the succah.

A 1663 woodcut illustrates a man building a shelter out of branches for the Jewish harvest festival of Succoth.

Another important part of the holiday is waving the lulav. The lulav is a bundle of branches from three trees that grow in Israel: palm, myrtle, and willow. The etrog (a lemon-like fruit) completes the grouping known as the Four Species.

Participants hold the lulav in one hand and the etrog in the other. When the two hands come together so the etrog touches the branches, the ceremony begins. People wave the lulav three times in each of the four cardinal directions (north, south, east, west), then up and down.

The lulav, the succah, and the blessings and songs reach across national and cultural boundaries. Jews may live in New York or New Delhi, India. They may speak different languages and salute different flags. Succoth becomes a symbolic ingathering, or bringing together. All over the world, Jews build little huts with thatched roofs. They gather the Four Species and perform the ancient rituals. By doing this, they affirm their links to one another and to the Jewish community as a whole.

Like all harvest festivals, Succoth has its symbols and rituals. A symbol is something that stands for something else, while a ritual is a ceremony that must be performed in a certain way.

The etrog, which looks like a lemon, is very important to Succoth. It symbolizes the people who both study the Torah and do good deeds.

For example, the Four Species of Succoth are symbols. The act of waving them is a ritual.

Symbols, Rituals, and Myths

History is often short on facts about the beginning of ancient rituals. When this happens, myth and folklore fill in the missing pieces with stories.

In Richmond, Virginia, high school students thatch the succah, or booth, for Succoth. Jews all over the world perform the same rituals with the same symbols, strengthening their ties to one another and their faith.

For example, in ancient Greece, a goat's horn overflowing with fruit, grain, and flowers was a symbol of abundance.

The story of how that came to be begins when the god Zeus was a child. A goat named Amalthea took care of him and fed him on her milk. Zeus loved to play with Amalthea, but he did not know his own strength. One day, he accidentally broke off one of her horns.

The Four Species of Succoth

The symbols and rituals of Succoth are filled with meaning. For example, each of the Four Species represent a different kind of person. The four together symbolize unity among all people, whatever their gifts or shortcomings.

The palm has taste but no fragrance: It represents those who study Torah but do not perform good deeds. The myrtle has fragrance but no taste: It represents those who do good deeds but do not study Torah. The willow has neither taste nor fragrance: It represents those who neither study Torah nor do good deeds. The etrog has both taste and fragrance: It represents those who study Torah and also perform good deeds.[1]

In Greek mythology, the king of the gods, Zeus, was cared for and fed by Amalthea the goat when he was a child. The Horn of Plenty evolved from the myth.

To apologize, Zeus promised Amalthea that the broken horn would always be filled with any kind of food she wanted. From that day, the Horn of Plenty, or cornucopia, gave abundance to anyone who owned it.[2]

The harvest myth of Borneo begins with barren fields and a great famine. Huminodun, daughter of the god Kinoingan, took pity on the starving

The Horn of Plenty, also called a cornucopia, is a symbol of abundance often seen during Thanksgiving, but it originated in ancient Greece.

people. The only way she knew to help them was to offer herself as a sacrifice.

She told her father to scatter pieces of her body over the fields. She promised that it would yield many good foods. There would be plenty for eating and seeds to save for the next planting time. Then she explained rituals that must be performed at the time of harvest.

When the scattering was done, the people were to leave the fields and not return for seven days and seven nights. Before the harvest, they were to stick seven stalks of rice into a bamboo stick and plant it at the center of the field.

After the harvest, they were to put the stick and the rice stalks into a storage basket. On the seventh day, a beautiful maiden stepped forth from the basket. She was Undul Ngadau, the spirit of Huminodun reborn.

The farmers of modern Borneo still perform these ancient rites, but they no longer expect the Unduk Ngadau, or harvest queen, to step out of her basket. Instead, every festival includes a pageant. Young women compete to see who best represents the beauty and the spirit of Huminodun. The winner becomes the Harvest Queen for that year.[3]

The pageant is the highlight of *Humabot*, the sixth and last ceremony of Borneo's harvest

Farmers dance and sing in celebration of Harvest Home, an old English harvest festival full of feasts and fun.

festival. It is a time of merrymaking, with dancing, traditional sports, and even a singing contest.

Fun, Feasting, and Games

Entertainment is an important part of harvest festivals. Some stress it more than others. For example, the Harvest Home celebrations of old England were noisy, jubilant, and filled with a spirit of fun.

A Song For Harvest Home

Harvest Home songs were simple and lively. One unnamed ditty summed up the work of farmers in just twenty-four words:

> Harvest-home, harvest-home.
>
> We have ploughed, we have sowed,
>
> We have reaped, we have mowed
>
> We have brought home every load,
>
> Hip, hip, hip, harvest-home.[4]

The celebration began when the reapers finished loading the last wagon. People climbed on top of the load, and off they would go, waving and shouting to anyone who could hear them. Others clasped hands and danced circles around the wagon. As the procession headed toward town, a piper marched in front, playing lively tunes.[5]

Even festivals that begin on a serious note have room for dancing, singing, feasting, and playing sports. For example, the Native American Green Corn Festival begins with prayers of thanksgiving and rituals of forgiveness. It continues with dancing, singing, feasting, and playing.[6]

Ball games are a special favorite, though each tribe has its own set of rules. For example, the

Iroquois take turns throwing a ball at a tall post. The player with the best elevation, or height, wins the game. The Yuchi set up baskets at both ends of a playing field. Two teams compete, trying to get the ball into the basket. The team with the most hits wins.[7]

The idea of games appears in harvest celebrations all over the world. Each game belongs to the culture that created it. The same is true of everything from the ingathering to the final feast.

Though the rituals differ from one culture to another, they share a common foundation. This would become important when Maulana Karenga set out to create Kwanzaa.

Dr. Martin Luther King, Jr., (1929–1968) led the civil rights movement, which sought equal rights for African Americans.

The Life of Maulana Karenga

The man who would be known as Maulana Karenga was born Ronald Everett on July 14, 1941. As the fourteenth child of a Baptist preacher, he grew up poor. As a victim of racism, he grew up angry.

In 1959, Ron Everett quit school and left Parsonsburg, Maryland, behind. He headed for Los Angeles, California. It turned out to be the right place and the right time to be young, black, and angry. The civil rights movement headed by Martin

The African-American Struggle for Civil Rights

The American civil rights movement began in the mid-1950s, with a boycott of racially segregated busses in Montgomery, Alabama. Led by Reverend Martin Luther King, Jr., African Americans refused to ride the city busses as long as they had to sit in the "colored" sections at the back.

The boycott lasted for more than a year, but on March 14, 1956, racial segregation on city busses was ruled unconstitutional. After that victory, the movement took on other segregated facilities, everything from public restrooms and water fountains to parks, lunch counters, and schools.

King himself became a genuine American hero. His accomplishments helped to make life better for Americans of all races.

Luther King, Jr., was still going strong; the protests and rebellions of the 1960s lay just ahead.

The Education of Ron Everett

Soon after arriving in California, Everett enrolled in Los Angeles City College (LACC), a two-year school that accepted high school dropouts. He proved to be an excellent student with a flair for leadership. He became active in student government, eventually becoming the first black student body president in LACC history. He also volunteered for social service projects in the black community.

Volunteering led to a personal high point— working with Malcolm X. To Everett, Malcolm was

In 1964, two of the most influential African Americans in modern history, Dr. Martin Luther King, Jr., and Malcolm X, wait together for a press conference. They were role models to the young Ronald Everett.

A Man Called X

Malcolm Little was born on May 19, 1925 in Omaha, Nebraska. He was one of eight children born to Earl and Louise Little. Being black defined Malcolm's childhood. When Malcolm was a baby, white racists drove his family out of Omaha; when he was four years old, another gang of racists burned down his home in Lansing, Michigan.

Earl Little died when Malcolm was six years old, and Louise Little had to be hospitalized for mental illness. Malcolm and his brothers and sisters went to different foster homes.

Malcolm grew up angry and rootless. He dropped out of school and took to a life of petty crime. In time, he went on to more serious offenses. By 1946, he was in prison, serving ten years for burglary.

It was there he discovered the teachings of Elijah Muhammad, founder of the Nation of Islam, a black nationalist religious organization. Malcolm became an enthusiastic convert, soon sealing his pledge to the Nation by dropping his last name. Unlike many black nationalists, Malcolm did not replace it with a Muslim or African surname. He chose "X" to honor the enslaved millions who had lost their family names, their culture, and their freedom.

Malcolm X broke with Elijah Muhammad in March 1964. On February 21, 1965, three members of the Nation of Islam broke through Malcolm's security and shot him down in a crowded auditorium.

more than a colleague; he was a role model and personal hero. When three assassins gunned Malcolm X down in New York City on February 21, 1965, Ron Everett did not know where to direct his outrage and anger.

He could not focus on racial enemies; the killers were black. As members of a group called the Nation of Islam (NOI), they considered Malcolm a traitor. He had left the NOI after disagreeing with the policies of its founder, Elijah Muhammad.

Just five months after the assassination of Malcolm X, another violent tragedy rocked the African-American community. It started in the Watts neighborhood of Los Angeles on a hot August night. A routine traffic stop got out of hand when a crowd began to gather. Before long, that crowd turned into a mob, and then the violence began. For six days, rioters burned buildings, looted shops and homes, and attacked innocent people, both black and white.

By the time the siege ended, Watts lay in ruins. According to reports made at the time, 34 people were killed, 1,032 injured, and 3,438 arrested. Property damage came to more than 40 million dollars.[1]

The scope of death and damage horrified Ron Everett. He could not go on with his studies as if

A man stands in front of the burnt remains of a store in the Watts neighborhood of Los Angeles, California. Many lost their lives, homes, and freedom during the riots in 1965.

nothing had happened. After finishing City College, he had earned a bachelor's degree at UCLA and was planning to go to graduate school for a master's degree. The Watts riots changed those plans. Everett quit school to devote himself to cultural and political activism.

Becoming Maulana Karenga

Becoming an activist was a life-changing decision and Ron Everett treated it as such. He Africanized his last name to Karenga, which means "keeper of traditions" in the Swahili language. For good measure, he adopted the title "Maulana," meaning "master teacher."

Karenga needed more than a title to become a master teacher; he needed followers who would turn to him for instruction and wisdom. To attract them, he founded an organization called "Us."

Some have claimed that Us stood for "United Slaves."[2] Historian Scot Brown says that Us is the pronoun "us," meaning black people as opposed to "them," meaning whites.[3] Karenga himself uses the pronoun rather than the initials.

The purpose of Us was to promote what Karenga called "cultural nationalism." This meant strengthening African-American culture by connecting with the lost traditions of the African past. It meant taking pride in being black. Karenga told Us members to "Think Black, Talk Black, Act Black, Create Black, Buy Black, Vote Black, and Live Black."[4]

Maulana Karenga, Us, and the Black Panthers

Not all black nationalists agreed with Maulana Karenga and the Us organization. For example, the Black Panthers held that reclaiming African culture was not enough. It would not stamp out racism or win the battle for equal rights. Only economic and political power could do that.

These viewpoints put Us and the Panthers on a collision course. The situation came to a head in 1969, when UCLA was establishing a new Afro-American Studies department. Us and the Panthers backed different candidates for director of the department. As the breach between them widened, members of both groups took to carrying guns on campus.

On January 17, 1969, a shootout left two Panthers dead and two Us members charged with murder. The following May, the Panthers denounced Karenga, saying that he did not

Maulana Karenga and the Black Panthers

The Black Panthers made quite a splash in the sixties. Founded in 1966 by college students Huey P. Newton and Bobby Seale, the Black Panthers wanted political power, and they were willing to fight for it.

The Panthers rejected Martin Luther King, Jr.'s quest for integration and racial equality; they wanted a separate black nation. They also rejected Maulana Karenga's cultural nationalism.

Culture, they said, was not enough. As Panther Fred Hampton put it, "Political power does not flow from the sleeve of a dashiki [traditional African garment]; political power flows from the barrel of a gun."[5]

Statements like this frightened the FBI and other government agencies. The Panthers became famous for trying to intimidate "the establishment." For example, in May 1967 the California state legislature was considering a gun control bill. To protest the bill, Bobby Seale marched into the legislative chamber with a fully armed group of Panthers at his back. The protestors did not change the legislature's vote, but they did draw public attention to their cause. In the process, they boosted black pride.

As black pride took hold, African Americans began looking at themselves differently. In the sixties African-American leaders worked for black power. "Black is beautiful," they declared, and black people began to listen. As pride and self-acceptance grew, so did interest in the African past. This created an environment in which Kwanzaa could grow and flourish.

represent "the best interests of the Black Liberation struggle."[6]

After the shootings, Karenga became tense and fearful. He suspected even his most loyal followers of plotting against him. In May 1970, Karenga believed that Us members Gail Davis and Deborah Jones were poisoning his food.

With two accomplices, he beat and tortured the women for their "sins." At trial, Judge Arthur L. Alarcon read from the psychiatric report. It noted that Karenga did strange things, "such as staring at the wall, talking to imaginary [people], claiming that he was attacked by dive-bombers and that his [lawyer] was in the next cell." Judge Alarcon sentenced Karenga to prison for one to ten years.[7]

Starting Over

By the time Karenga got out of prison in 1975, he had regained control of his mind. The next thing he had to do was regain control of his life. This meant finishing his education, rebuilding Us, and promoting Kwanzaa to African-American communities throughout the nation.

Slowly, he put everything back together. In 1976, he earned a Ph.D. in Political Science from the United States University in San Diego,

Ronald Everett, the political and cultural activist also known as Maulana Karenga, stands outside a courtroom in Los Angeles, California, in 1971.

In 2004, Dr. Maulana Karenga gave a lecture on the significance of Kwanzaa at Clemson University in South Carolina.

California. His work brought professional and personal success. In 1986, he became chairman of Black Studies at California State University, Long Beach. By the turn of the twenty-first century, the holiday he created in 1966 had a life of its own. As many as 15 million people celebrated it each year.[8]

Rosa Parks (1913–2005) refused to give up her seat to a white person o a bus in 1955. Her action started a boycott of the Montgomery, Alabam bus system and helped give rise to the civil rights movement.

Kwanzaa and African-American Culture

For African Americans, freedom from slavery did not mean freedom from racism. Black people lived in segregated neighborhoods and sent their children to segregated schools. Often the only jobs open to black workers were those that white workers did not want.

Forced to the fringes of mainstream culture, African Americans built a cultural life of their own. They did it on the farms and in the country towns of the South and in the ghettos of northern cities.

Black churches, schools, lodges, businesses, charity organizations, and places of entertainment existed alongside their white counterparts.

Black leaders developed in these communities. Some of them built reputations that extended into white society. For example, in the early 1900s, agricultural chemist George Washington Carver discovered three hundred uses for the lowly peanut.[1] Because of his discoveries, peanuts became an important cash crop that benefited everyone.

Dr. Charles Drew developed a method for safe blood transfusions. His work saved countless lives. Musicians like Scott Joplin, Louis Armstrong, and Bessie Smith made music that crossed racial boundaries.

Connecting to the African Heritage

These people and others like them gave black Americans cause for pride, but they could not link them to the African past. Slave owners had long since stripped much of that past away by forcing slaves to take American names and forbidding them to use African languages, customs, or traditions.

By the time slavery ended, most black people had lost touch with their African past. Some knew little or nothing about their American past. They had no birth certificates recording when and where they were born, and no last names to connect them to particular families.

The names they adopted after emancipation, being set free from slavery, had nothing to do with their personal histories. Some took the name of a former master. Others picked historical names like Washington or Jefferson. Still others used biblical names or simply picked something that sounded good.

During the 1960s, a new generation of black people confronted the issue of names. Like Malcolm X, many disliked the "slave names" they had acquired. They wanted something of their own, something that was not borrowed from white people. Some converted to the Islamic faith and took Muslim names. For example, basketball great Kareem Abdul Jabbar was born Lew Alcindor. Boxer Muhammad Ali was once known as Cassius Clay. Some followed Ron Everett's example and took African names.

Some cultural nationalists were not content with African names; they wanted to reclaim the African past as their ethnic heritage. They soon found that walking the walk, talking the talk, and dressing in African cloth did not turn them into

Alex Haley and Roots

"Early in the spring of 1750, in the village of Juffure, four days upriver from the coast of The Gambia, West Africa, a manchild was born to Omoro and Binta Kinte."[2]

With these words, writer Alex Haley began the story that would become *Roots: The Saga of an American Family*. This newborn manchild was Kunta Kinte, the ancestor who linked Alex Haley's family to its African past.

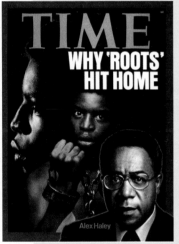
Alex Haley

Alex Haley grew up hearing these stories from relatives who believed that this long-ago African was a real person. As an adult, Alex Haley did not want to settle for belief. He wanted to know. His search for Kunta Kinte took ten years. He traced the family back through generations of free people, then through generations of slaves. The trail ended on the Atlantic coast, where slave ships once docked to sell their human cargo.

Haley got the names of slave ships that landed in America and traced them back to their points of origin in Africa. From there, he traced back to the village of Juffure, where a griot (gree-OH), or oral historian, recited the name of Kunta Kinte, born to Omoro and Binta Kinte in a long-ago springtime.[3]

Haley chronicled this story in his bestselling book *Roots: The Saga of an American Family*. In 1977, *Roots* became an enormously successful television miniseries. Its impact crossed racial divides as millions of American viewers confronted the horrors of slavery.

Africans. However, it did help them reclaim their identities as African Americans.

"African American" is the latest name to describe Americans of African origin. They have also been called "Negro," "colored," and "black."

Booker T. Washington (1856-1915) was an important black political leader who advised Presidents Theodore Roosevelt and William Howard Taft on racial policies and founded a vocational school for blacks in Tuskegee, Alabama.

Booker T. Washington
"I've Got a Name"

"From the time when I could remember anything, I had been called simply 'Booker.' Before going to school it had never occurred to me that it was needful or appropriate to have an additional name. When I heard the school-roll called, I noticed that all of the children had at least two names, and some of them indulged in what seemed to me the extravagance of having three. I was in deep perplexity, because I knew that the teacher would demand of me at least two names, and I had only one. By the time the occasion came for the enrolling of my name, an idea occurred to me which I thought would make me equal to the situation; and so, when the teacher asked me what my full name was, I calmly told him 'Booker Washington,' as if I had been called by that name all my life; and by that name I have since been known. Later in my life I found that my mother had given me the name of 'Booker Taliaferro' soon after I was born, but in some way that part of my name seemed to disappear and for a long while was forgotten, but as soon as I found out about it I revived it, and made my full name 'Booker Taliaferro Washington.' I think there are not many men in our country who have had the privilege of naming themselves in the way that I have."[4]

These names did not replace one another in an orderly fashion. In the early twentieth century, "Negro" and "colored" were common. By the 1960s, they were considered derogatory, or insulting. Yet the National Association for the Advancement of Colored People (NAACP) has kept the name its founders selected.

"Black" became popular with the black nationalists of the 1960s and 1970s. By the 1980s, "African American" had come into general favor. It describes Americans of African ancestry in much the same way that Mexican American or Italian American describes Americans of these ancestries. "Black" is a racial term, describing all people of African ancestry, regardless of their national or cultural background.[6]

Kwanzaa and the African-American Middle Class

The civil rights movement and the activism of the 1960s and 1970s paved the way for many African Americans to enter the middle class. They went to college or trade school, found good jobs, and bought nice homes.

In spite of these achievements, middle-class African Americans faced a newer, quieter form of racism. They made less money than whites and

About Africa

Africa is not a nation—it is a continent, one of seven major landmasses on earth. Sub-Sahara Africa, or "black Africa" as it is sometimes called, has some fifty nations. They are populated by many different tribal groups, each with its own culture and even its own language. Scholars estimate that sub-Sahara Africa has about 1,000 different languages.[5]

Geography helps to create these cultural differences. Sub-Sahara Africa has rain forests and broad grassland prairies called savannas. It has greenbelts, where the soil and climate are suitable for farming.

The rain forest is warm and moist, teeming with plant and animal life. There is plenty of rain, and it leaves fine mists hovering in the air long after the clouds have passed. Even when there are no rain clouds, the forest is a place of shadows. Giant trees with thick, leafy branches create a canopy that filters out the sunlight.

Nothing filters out sunlight on the savanna. The Kalahari has almost no trees, only bushes and prairie grass. For much of the year, it has no surface water. Rivers, streams, lakes, and ponds fill during the rainy season, then go dry in the bright, baking sun.

The savanna and the rain forest do have one thing in common; both lend themselves to the hunter-gatherer way of life. People lived as nomads, with the men hunting for meat and the women collecting edible plants. Agricultural tribes lived and worked in the greenbelt, shaping their lives around the rhythms of sowing and reaping. These were the people whose festivals would inspire Maulana Karenga to create Kwanzaa.

Map of Africa

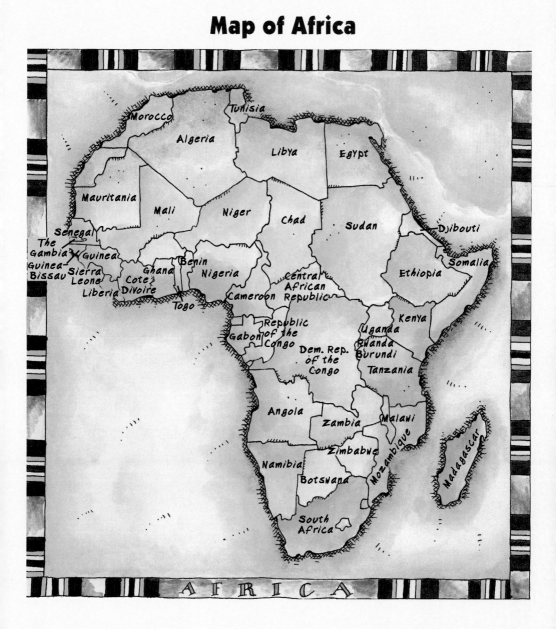

had less chance of becoming top-level executives. Many had escaped the inner-city ghettos, but still faced limited choices when they tried to rent an apartment or buy a home. According to sociologist Mary Pattillo-McCoy, real estate agents and apartment managers "steer middle-class blacks into already established African American neighborhoods."[7]

Thus, there was a white middle class and a black middle class. They existed side by side, but rarely interacted with one another. African Americans built their own social networks, often copying them from white culture.

Kwanzaa offered them an African alternative for the Christmas and New Year season. Black radicals had developed the holiday, but it was the black middle class that kept it alive. Maulana Karenga realized that this broader popularity would weaken Kwanzaa's revolutionary spirit. He also realized that this was the price of survival. He acknowledged this in his 1988 book on celebrating the holiday: "Kwanzaa has become a vital part of the lives of millions of African Americans who may or may not be in the movement but . . . are very interested in and committed to Kwanzaa."[8]

In 1968, Olympic gold and bronze medallists Tommie Smith (center) and John Carlos raise their fists in racial protest during the American national anthem. Although the civil rights movement improved the lives of many African Americans, they still suffered discrimination and prejudice.

He did not extend this welcome to non-blacks. Neither did many of the people who organized celebrations in their communities. Then in 1993, an incident in Roxbury, Massachusetts, brought the situation to public attention.

It began when a white mother came to the community Kwanzaa celebration with her eight-year-old biracial son. One of the organizers told her to leave; Kwanzaa was for black people only, he said. The little boy broke down in tears as his mother took him by the hand and made a quick retreat.

This triggered an outburst of protest. Some pointed out that Kwanzaa was supposed to be about culture and tradition, not about race. Therefore, barring people on the basis of race did not make sense. Some African Americans took this to heart and began welcoming non-blacks to their public celebrations.

By the twenty-first century, the official Kwanzaa website reinforced this openness: "Any . . . message that is good for a particular people . . . speaks not just to that people, it speaks to the world. The principles of Kwanzaa and the message of Kwanzaa has a universal message for all people of good will."[9]

Kwanzaa Comes Into its Own

As Kwanzaa grew, it became well known to African Americans and others. Teachers included it in their lesson plans. The U.S. Postal Service issued commemorative stamps. Greeting card companies designed cards for people to send to one another. The media began wishing people "Happy Kwanzaa" along with "Merry Christmas" and "Happy Hanukkah."

Today, African-American communities hold public celebrations of the holiday. Planning committees begin working on Kwanzaa events months in advance. They hold workshops and develop a schedule of tasks that leads right up to the holiday. Even when the holiday is over, they do not let down. Organizers simply go back to the beginning, planning for next year.

One Kwanzaa guidebook recommends a seminar in February as "an annual follow-up" to the celebration.[11] It should summarize the past event and identify areas that need improvement. It should also lay the foundation for organizing the next Kwanzaa celebration.

In addition to this organizing work, people who are serious about Kwanzaa must learn the meaning of its symbols and the proper way to

Another African-American Celebration

On June 19, 1865, Union troops under the command of Major General George Granger landed at Galveston, Texas. He carried news of the Confederate surrender and the end of the American civil war. He also carried General Order Number 3, which he read aloud to the assembled Texans: "The people of Texas are informed that in accordance with a Proclamation from [President Abraham Lincoln], all slaves are free. This [means] absolute equality of rights . . . between former masters and slaves, and the connection . . . between them becomes that between employer and free laborer."[10]

Jubilation followed, and the news spread. Only later did the former slaves learn that President Abraham Lincoln had issued the Emancipation Proclamation on the first day of January, 1863. The news of freedom had reached them two and a half years after the fact.

Over time, "June nineteenth" got shortened to "Juneteenth," and spread beyond Texas. Today, it stands as the oldest known celebration of freedom from slavery and grows in popularity every year.

In 1997, the U.S. Postal Service issued a commemorative stamp honoring the African-American community thanks to the efforts of Jose Ferrer (right), the chairman of the Kwanzaa Holiday Foundation.

conduct its rituals. They must study the seven principles and find ways to integrate them into daily life.

Not everyone is willing to devote this kind of effort to the holiday. Many people will attend events but will not help coordinate them. They will take part in rituals but will not study the principles behind them.

Even this limited participation has value. Kwanzaa binds people to the community and gives them pride in their ancestry. It exposes them to the principles of a meaningful life.

Kwanzaa Around the World

Kwanzaa's success in the United States has caught the interest of people of African descent in other countries. It is becoming popular in Canada, England, the Caribbean, and other places.

Other countries add their own touch to the holiday. For example, Canadians call it an African-Canadian holiday. They use people and events from Canadian history to help explain the principles of the holiday. For example, they illustrate "purpose" with Mary Bibb, an African Canadian who published an anti-slavery newspaper in 1851. For "faith" they mentioned the deep faith of the runaway slaves who found refuge in Canada.[12]

In Nottingham, England, the African and Caribbean communities have been celebrating Kwanzaa since the early 1970s. Like the Canadians, they draw on their own background, marking the celebrations with the art, music, food, and customs of their homeland.

Several islands in the Caribbean hold Kwanzaa celebrations. For example, in the United States Virgin Islands, a women's social organization has been sponsoring Kwanzaa events since 1995. Their celebrations have a multicultural flavor due to their varied backgrounds. For example, many celebrations begin with four different anthems: the American National Anthem, the Virgin Islands March, the Black National Anthem ("Lift Every Voice and Sing"), and the South African anthem.[13]

This openness to many traditions has made Kwanzaa a unifying force for black people. It lets them share their differences and celebrate the African heritage that binds them together.

The seven candles in the
kinara symbolize the seven
principles of Kwanzaa.

Symbols, Rituals, and Traditions

Kwanzaa takes its name from *matunda ya kwanza*, meaning "first fruits" in the Swahili language. This term refers to the ingathering of crops at harvest season.

Though Kwanzaa uses the structure of harvest festivals, it does not focus on crops. According to Maulana Karenga, people of African ancestry are the "living human harvest" of Kwanzaa.[1] The holiday gathers them together to share their common heritage.

Karenga identified five activities that harvest festivals share: ingathering, giving reverence to the creator and creation, honoring the past, bonding with the community, and celebrating all that is good in life.

Rituals and symbols give meaning to these activities. A ritual is a ceremonial action or series of actions. A symbol is usually an object that represents an idea or quality.

The Seven Symbols

Kwanzaa uses simple, everyday objects to illustrate its principles: a place mat; a candle holder with seven branches; candles; ears of corn; a basket of fruit; nuts and vegetables; a unity cup; and gifts. Each has special meaning.

Mkeka, the place mat, represents the historical and cultural foundations of African life. It should be placed on the floor or a low table. The other symbols go on top of it.

Some families get together to make their own mkeka. They start by choosing a material, usually straw, or African cloth. Everyone helps to create the design and apply the decorations.

Kinara, the candle holder, belongs in the middle of the mkeka, and stands for the African

The Seven Symbols

Name	Translation	Pronunciation	Symbolism
Mkeka	Straw mat	m-KAY-kah	Cultural foundation
Kinara	Candle holder	kee-NAH-rah	The ancestors
Mishumaa Saba	Candles	mee-shoo-MA-ah SAH-bah	The seven principles of Kwanzaa
Muhindi	Ears of corn	moo-HEEN-dee	Children
Mazao	Crops	mah-ZAH-oh	The fruits of labor
Kikombe	Unity cup	kee-KOOAM-bay	Unity
Zawadi	Gifts	sah-WAH-dee	Sharing

ancestors. It can be made of many materials, in many shapes, so long as it has seven branches coming from one base. This design symbolizes the unity of African people the world over.

Mishumaa Saba, the seven candles, go into the kinara. A single black candle in the middle stands for the African people. To the right, three red candles symbolize the struggle for freedom and self-determination. To the left, three green candles

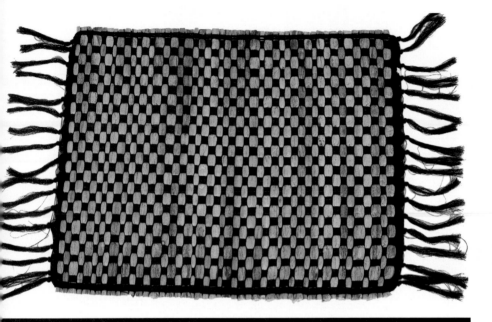

The mkeka represents the foundations of African culture and the other symbols are placed on top of it.

celebrate the living earth and the future of black people everywhere.

The colors come from the pan-African flag. This flag does not belong to a particular nation. It belongs to all people of African ancestry, wherever in the world they might live.

Mishumaa Saba also stand for the seven days and seven principles of the holiday. For example, lighting the black candle on the first day stands for the principle of unity.

Muhindi, the ears of corn, represent a staple, or basic, crop in Africa. It is essential to the local diet, especially for poor people who cannot afford a variety of foods. Failure of other crops may be a serious problem. Failure of the corn crop can easily become a disaster.

Because corn is so important, African Americans place fresh-picked ears of it on the mkeka. There should be one ear for every child in

Each child in the home receives an ear of corn (muhindi) placed on the mkeka.

Celebrating Yams

Ghana's yam festival is called *Homowo,* which means "to hoot at hunger." Because yams are so important to the local diet, a good harvest is cause for celebration, along with a great deal of singing, dancing, and drumming.

The festival begins with an ingathering, as families bring the first fruits of harvest to the village. The chief blesses the harvest, the community thanks the spirits of earth and sky for it, and the celebration begins.

A high point of the festival is an enormous feast, featuring dishes made with yams. People bake, broil, roast, fry, and mash yams. They make yam soup and even yam flour.

The chiefs from different villages in Ghana throw cornmeal onto the ground in celebration of Homowo.

All these activities make the Homowo a fun and fitting end to the growing season. People return to their ordinary lives and to the fields which must be prepared for another year's crop of yams.

the home. Even people without children put two ears on the mkeka. This is because African tradition holds everyone responsible for the children of the community.[2]

Mazao, the crops, are usually arranged in a basket that makes a colorful display on the mkeka. They symbolize the first fruits for which Kwanzaa is named and recall the African festivals that served as its model.

Kikombe, the unity cup, stands for solidarity among all people of African descent. This includes deceased family members and unknown ancestors. There is no standard design for the cup. It can be purchased or handmade, so long as it is both beautiful and useful.

Like the candles in the kinara, the unity

The kikombe symbolizes unity among all black people, even those who are no longer living. It will be used throughout the seven-day celebration.

Zawadi are useful gifts, many handmade, which reflect Kwanzaa or African heritage.

cup is used throughout the celebration. Every day it sits on the mkeka; every day the people share it and pour libations to honor the ancestors.

Zawadi, the gifts, are not like ordinary presents. In some way, they should symbolize Kwanzaa or black culture. Handmade items are especially prized. People with a knack for crafts often make kinaras, mkekas, or kikombes for gifts.

Rituals for Seven Days

During Kwanzaa, people focus on their African heritage. They wear African-style clothes, eat African-style foods, and even greet one another in a special way. They also perform rituals, ceremonies that set the holiday apart from ordinary life.

A Libation Statement

Our fathers and mothers came here, lived, loved, struggled, and built here. At this place, their love and lives and labor rose like the sun and gave strength and meaning to the day. For them, who have so much, we give in return. On this same sod we will sow our seeds and build and move in unity and strength. Here too, we will continue their struggle for liberation and a higher level of human life. May our eyes be like the eagle, our strength be like the elephant, and the boldness of our life be like the lion. And may we remember and honor our ancestors and the legacy they left for as long as the sun shines and the waters flow.

Instead of hello, they say *"Habari gani"* (ha-BAR-ee-gani), which means "What's the news?" The answer is the principle of the day. For example, on the first day of Kwanzaa the reply to "Habari gani" would be *"Umoja"* (unity).[3]

Each night of Kwanzaa, everyone performs the *harambee* (hah-RAM-beh) ritual. Harambee is a Swahili word meaning "let's pull together."

Seven Candles, Seven Days

Day 1: Light the black candle for unity.

Day 2: Light the red candle next to the black for self-determination.

Day 3: Light the green candle next to the black for collective work and responsibility.

Day 4: Light the middle red candle for cooperative economics.

Day 5: Light the middle green candle for purpose.

Day 6: Light the end red candle for creativity.

Day 7: Light the end green candle for faith.[4]

Participants dramatize it by raising the right arm, hand open. Then they pull down, while closing the hand into a fist. Along with the gesture, everyone repeats "harambee" seven times, in honor of the Nguzo Saba, the seven principles.

Tambiko (tahm-BEE-koh), the opening libation, pays tribute to the African ancestors. A respected elder pours wine in each of the four directions (north, south, east, west), then passes the cup around so everyone can drink.

While older people offer the libation, children light the candles. On the first night, they light the black candle of unity. Every night afterward, they light another candle for another principle. They also re-light the earlier candles so the kinara glows more brightly each day.

Rituals shape the celebration with familiar words and gestures. This becomes a framework for cultural activities such as singing, dancing, drumming, and storytelling. Kwanzaa has helped many African Americans get in touch with this part of their heritage.

To the African ancestors, songs and stories were more than entertainment; they were substitutes for written language. People known as *griots* memorized the history, culture, and family

A Griot's Story

"I am, first of all, an African from Senegal. . . . I come from a family of musicians or griots. We griots are simultaneously musicians, historians and singers, and our art is handed down from father to son and from generation to generation. . . . Since writing [did not exist] in some parts of Africa, it was necessary to entrust a social group with the task of reciting history, and thus of acting as the memory of the African people. . . . I know a story about a gathering of griots in Mali. I believe it is true, since many people were eyewitnesses to it. Every seven years, the great griots of Mali met to repair the roof of a hut. They sang and played music at the same time, whereupon the roof flew up into the air as if by [magic] and landed on the ground. They restored the roof. Then they started singing again, and the roof rose up from the ground and settled on the hut."[5]

—Lamine Konte

ancestry of their communities. They brought history to life with songs and stories.

Griots still exist today, singing their songs and telling their stories. They preserve tradition for new generations so that the spirit of the ancestors will not be lost. In this goal, the ancient tradition of the griot meets the new tradition of Kwanzaa.

In Washington, D.C., an Elder leads the harambee ritual for Kwanzaa.

The Principles
of Kwanzaa

Each year when Kwanzaa ends, everyone packs away the mkekas, kinaras, and African robes. They do not, however, pack away the Nguzo Saba. The seven principles are not just for the holiday; they are a way of life.

Like the African cultures that inspired them, the principles are down-to-earth and practical. They deal with strong families and communities, making a living, and finding creative solutions to everyday problems.

Nguzo Saba: The Seven Principles

Day/Name	Pronunciation	Meaning
1. Umoja	oo-MO-jah	Unity
2. Kujichagulia	koo-jee-cha-GOO-lee-ah	Self-determination
3. Ujima	oo-JEE-mah	Collective work and responsibility
4. Ujamaa	oo-jah-MAH-ah	Cooperative economics
5. Nia	NEE-ah	Purpose
6. Kuumba	koo-OOM-bah	Creativity
7. Imani	ee-MAH-nee	Faith

The First Principle: Umoja (Unity)

It is no accident that unity is the first principle of Kwanzaa.

Generations of black leaders have recognized the need for Africans to come together as a people. This is why the call for harambee, pulling together, begins on the first night of Kwanzaa and threads through the whole celebration.

Umoja begins with the ritual greeting "Habari gani?" (what's the news?), to which the people reply "Umoja." Other rituals follow, such as affirming harambee, lighting the candles, and paying tribute to the ancestors. The tribute begins with the libation. Then the group discusses ancestors who practiced Umoja in their lives. For example, Martin Luther King, Jr., unified the black people of Montgomery, Alabama. Together these ordinary citizens launched the bus boycott that would shape the civil rights movement of the 1950s.

After forty years of Kwanzaa celebrations, Martin Luther King, Jr., and other famous ancestors have been honored many times. Because of this, some groups choose lesser-known people. In her book on celebrating Kwanzaa, Jessica B. Harris picked interesting people from different

Symbols from a Kwanzaa celebration in New York remain on display. The Nguzo Saba are principles that should be followed all year around, not just during Kwanzaa.

parts of the world: Kwame Nkrumah helped the nation of Ghana win independence from England. Mae Aninha was a leading figure in the candomblé religion of Brazil, Marcus Garvey of Jamaica formed a "back to Africa" movement in the 1920s; African-American educator Mary McLeod Bethune founded the National Council for Negro Women in 1935.[1]

With these people as models, conversation turns to individual plans. Guests talk about ways to encourage unity in their homes, communities, and places of work.

The Second Principle: Kujichagulia (Self-determination)

The second principle of Kwanzaa affirms the African-American struggle "to define ourselves, name ourselves, create for ourselves, and speak for ourselves instead of being defined, named, created, and spoken for by others."[2]

On the night of *Kujichagulia*, celebrants light the first red candle in the kinara. They talk about self-determination and what it means to them. They tell of Africans and African Americans who took charge of their own lives and achieved success.

Popular subjects include historical figures like Shaka Zulu, the warrior-king who fought for freedom in nineteenth-century Africa. Modern favorites can range from former Secretary of State Colin Powell to talk-show host Oprah Winfrey or basketball legend Michael Jordan.

In African thought, self-determination and group unity are not at odds with one another. A unified community supports its members, and in turn draws strength from their achievements.

The Third Principle: Ujima (Collective Work and Responsibility)

The theme of unity carries over into the third principle. *Ujima* focuses on working together and sharing responsibility for the needs of the community. It means putting cooperation ahead of competition.

On the night of Ujima, celebrants light the first green candle. They discuss ways to work together and help one another. They tell about black people who have made their communities better places to live.

Some of these people paid a heavy price for their activities. Jomo Kenyatta spent seven years in prison because of his work for black Africans in

An African-American community performs the libation, drinking ceremoniously to their ancestors' accomplishments.

Kenya. Fannie Lou Hamer was jailed and beaten many times because she helped black people in Mississippi register to vote.

The Fourth Principle: Ujamaa (Cooperative Economics)

While *Ujima* focuses on building strong communities, Ujamaa deals with building strong economies. In a typically African way, the principle of Ujamaa calls for a group effort. Communities work to achieve prosperity for everyone.

The struggle for economic health begins with African-American business. New businesses enrich the community. They create jobs for black workers and resources for black consumers. When people work and buy in their own neighborhoods, profits stay at home. Over time, even small purchases can add up to big differences. For example, five dollars spent at the corner store directly benefits the local economy. The same five dollars spent at a supermarket across town does not.

People discuss these things on the night of Ujamaa. Some explore the idea of starting a new business. Others resolve to spend their money locally whenever possible.

Not everyone who makes these resolutions will follow through. Success requires more than bright ideas and good intentions. It requires hard work and a sense of purpose.

The Fifth Principle: Nia (Purpose)

On the night of *Nia*, celebrants gather to discuss their goals as individuals and as members of the community. Setting goals gives purpose to life and inspires action.

People who know where they are going and why have a better chance of reaching their destination. Purpose pulls them toward their goals. It helps them set priorities or rank ideas according to their importance. That in turn helps them avoid wasting time on things that do not matter.

As part of Nia, people discuss Africans and African Americans who lived purpose-driven lives. They talk about people like Marian Wright Edelman, who founded the Children's Defense Fund to help underprivileged children. They talk about attorney Thurgood Marshall, who argued the Supreme Court case that ended racial segregation in America's public schools.

The Sixth Principle: Kuumba (Creativity)

Creativity is not limited to artists, actors, or musicians. Everyone has imagination and special talents that can help the community. A business-person who finds a way to lower costs or increase profits is being creative, as is a cook who invents a new recipe, or a mechanic who tracks down an engine problem that nobody else could find.

On the night of *Kuumba*, people light the second-to-last candle and celebrate creativity in all its forms. This is the time of the *Karamu*, the great feast. People gather to talk, eat, and share the music, art, and literature of African cultures.

The Seventh Principle: Imani (Faith)

Imani wraps up the holiday with a focus on faith. Because Kwanzaa is a cultural holiday, the celebration of faith is not connected to any particular religion. Maulana Karenga called upon African Americans to "believe with all our heart in our Creator, our people, our parents, our teachers, our leaders and the righteousness and victory of our struggle."[3]

This description allows for individual differences. Religious people might emphasize faith in God, while others concentrate on faith in community leaders or social institutions. This is one of the strengths of Kwanzaa; it speaks to people in many different ways.

In Charlotte, North Carolina, a woman
performs an African dance during Kwanzaa.

6

Celebrating Kwanzaa Today

When Kwanzaa began in 1966, it had symbols, principles, and rituals in place, enough to fill the seven days. The only thing it did not have was a history. Nobody grew up with Kwanzaa. Parents did not have fond holiday memories to share with their children. Children could not look forward to something they did not understand.

By the twenty-first century, Kwanzaa was becoming more familiar. People born after 1966 have fond memories of Kwanzaa. They accepted it as naturally as their elders accepted Thanksgiving or Memorial Day. They have built Kwanzaa memories that carry from one year to the next, making each one more special than the last.

How to Celebrate Kwanzaa

Like all large gatherings, a community Kwanzaa takes planning and hard work. Preparations start weeks, even months, in advance. Organizers have

In Los Angeles, California, drummers and dancers perform to celebrate the first day of Kwanzaa.

The African Pledge

We are an Afrikan [sic] People!!

We will remember the humanity, glory and sufferings of our ancestors.

We will honor the struggles of our elders.

We will strive to bring new values and new life to our people.

We will have peace and harmony among us.

We will be loving, sharing and creative.

We will work, study and listen so we may learn, learn so we may teach.

We will cultivate self reliance.

We will struggle to resurrect and unify our homeland.

We will raise many children for our nation.

We will have discipline, patience, devotion and courage. We will live as models to provide new directions for our people.

We will be free and self-determining.

We are Afrikan people

And we will win.[1]

to find a place for the event, recruit helpers, plan a program, and arrange for entertainment and food. The pace speeds up as the day draws closer. Volunteers hang flags, banners, and streamers of

In Oxford, Mississippi, school children join in as a storyteller shares stories and songs from around the world during a Black History Month program. African fables and songs are used to illustrate the seven principles of Kwanzaa.

red, black, and green. They arrange displays of African arts and handicrafts and set up the mkeka.

On December 26, Kwanzaa begins. Kwanzaa still follows the basic format that Maulana Karenga created in 1966. Ceremonies open with a welcome to the guests and a libation to honor the ancestors. Next comes the harambee ritual, followed by candle lighting. Many groups include the African Pledge, a statement of solidarity and faith in the African-American future. After that, the host or an elder introduces and explains the principle of the day.

The guests explore this principle through songs, stories, discussions, and other activities. The program focuses on African and African-American culture. Singers, dancers, drummers, and storytellers offer entertainment with an African theme.

Both home and community celebrations have a place during Kwanzaa; people do not have to choose between them. Many communities gather on the first night to get the holiday off to a good start. The Karamu feast is also a favorite time for communities to get together. When there is no community celebration, families gather in their homes.

An African Story

African griots often used stories to make a point about ethics or values. This story from the Alur people deals with generosity of spirit. It illustrates self-determination, showing the unexpected benefits of making wise and humane decisions.

The Unlucky Boy

One day, two boys went out from the village to catch birds for supper. Both laid their snares carefully, in the way they had been taught. The first boy caught a fine, fat pigeon and took it home for his mother to cook. The second boy was not so lucky; he caught only a spider. Because the spider would not be good to eat, he set it free.

The next day the boys went out again and set their snares as carefully as before. The first boy caught a guinea-fowl, which would make a fine supper for his family. The second boy found a bolt of lightning tangled in his snare. Because lightning would not be good to eat, he untangled the bolt and threw it back to the sky.

Now it happened that the king told the boys to cut new grinding-stones for his flour mill. Neither knew how to do this, but together they tried to hew a proper grinding-stone out of living rock. All they did was blunt their axes.

The boys were at their wits' end when the unlucky one remembered the lightning bolt he set free from his snare. "Lightning," he called, "come and help me."

And the lightning came; flashing, thundering, striking the rock again and again, cutting off perfect grinding stones. The king was so pleased by this that he gave the boys another task; to bring down a star from the sky.

Neither one of the boys knew where to start. They were sure that this time they would fail the king, and draw his wrath down upon them. Then the unlucky boy remembered the spider he set free from his snare. "Spider," he called, "come and help me."

And the spider came.

"I need a star from the sky," said the boy.

The spider set to work, weaving a web that stretched from earth into the sky. Then he scrambled up the web and took a star down from the sky.

The king rewarded the boy with many cows and baskets of food. So it was that the boy's generosity to a lightning bolt and a spider changed his luck from bad to good. And so it was that he became rich and respected and was never again called the unlucky boy.

Home celebrations are often simpler and more informal than public ones. Much depends on the size of the gathering. A small family might settle for lighting the candles and discussing the principle of the day at the dinner table. An extended family gathering with siblings, cousins, aunts, uncles, and in-laws would be more elaborate.

Candles and History

Whatever size the celebration, planners can be creative. They can design new activities or find new ways to express familiar ideas. For example, a religious education director in Massachusetts built a dramatic history lesson around the candles in the kinara:

> The Kwanzaa candles are seven—three red, a black, and three green. The black candle is a celebration of being black. . . . It is a candle of the present, of today. The green candles are vision candles—candles of hopes, dreams, and promises for the future. The red candles are struggle candles, past candles, candles the color of blood, candles the color of courage. All seven candles help African Americans to remember a long struggle against injustice . . . and to promise each other that they will continue to work together against injustice. As a white person, I can't be

a part of the remembering or the promise. I will not light the candles, for they are not mine to light. I will, however, honor the struggle for justice by speaking a history—the story of a people which is not often enough told in our society.

The leader asked one person to stand: "You represent the first generation of West African people who came to this world in slavery, coming in the year 1619 to Jamestown."

Another person stood beside the first: "You represent the children of those people, born between 1625 and 1650, and you remain enslaved."

And so it went, with each person standing for a generation. The line grew through revolutions, wars, civil rights, and black power. The fifteenth and last person stood for today's generation: "It is up to [you] to retell the story of the past, to understand the struggle, to have dreams about the future."[2]

Walking the Parachute

At a community Kwanzaa in Louisville, Kentucky, a group of men brought a large package into the room and laid it on the floor. While everyone watched, they unwrapped a parachute. At a signal, the adults circled around the parachute and picked it up. The children formed a line. While the adults held tight to the parachute, the children walked across it, one by one. Every adult had to do his or her part or one of the children would have a nasty fall.

The exercise illustrated an African proverb: it takes a village to raise a child.[3] Both children and adults seemed nervous at first, but the children walked, the adults held tight, and soon people were laughing and joking.

Karamu: The Feast

The Karamu is a high point of the Kwanzaa celebration. Over the years, people have added their own special touches. The Black Students Alliance at Rensselaer Polytechnic Institute in Troy, New York, holds potluck dinners. Some groups experiment with as many different African dishes as possible.

College professor Jessica B. Harris turned the Karamu into a "healing supper." She wanted to create "a communal meal that opens the gates of remembrance through food and speaks of our history, our past, and our hopes for the future."[4]

The act of eating becomes a ritual. With each course, one of the guests reads about the cultural importance of that particular food. For example, with fish someone may read, "The water deep. The water wide. The water profound."[5] With dessert,

January 1 marks both the end of Kwanzaa and the beginning of a new year. The lessons learned and promises made during the holiday are now ready to be incorporated into everyday life.

the reading focuses on hope and the sweetness of life.

Last Things

When the feasting is over, the day of ending arrives. People review the lessons of the past week and prepare for the return to ordinary life. This day is doubly important, marking both the end of Kwanzaa and the beginning of a brand new year. Everyone has explored the principles and made plans for the future. Now comes the hard part—putting those plans into action to build stronger individuals, families, and communities.

Not-So-Famous Tribute Poem

There are a lot of "not-so-famous" people who have helped shape our lives. They can be family, friends, teachers, and coaches. They can be people who have invented something that we use every day or who have somehow made a difference to our society. Think about who has the greatest influence in your life. If you wish, go to the library or, with an adult's permission, go on the Internet to do some research.

Once you have thought about a not-so-famous person, honor them by writing a tribute poem. Share your poem and your thoughts about that person with family and friends.

abundance—A large quantity.

anthem—A patriotic song of praise for one's country.

convert—A person who has changed from one belief, religion, or view to another.

emancipation—Setting free from slavery.

harvest festival—A festival celebrated usually in the autumn after the harvest.

heritage—Something that comes to one from one's ancestors.

ingathering—To gather in.

integration—An act to form as a whole, unite.

libation—An act of pouring a liquid as a sacrifice to a god or goddess; an act of drinking ceremoniously.

racism—Racial prejudice and discrimination.

ritual—An established form for a ceremony.

segregation—Enforced separation of a race, class, or group.

Swahili—A Bantu language that is a trade and governmental language in much of East Africa and the Congo region.

symbol—Something that stands for something else.

tradition—The handing down of information, beliefs, or customs from one generation to another.

CHAPTER NOTES

◆ **Chapter 1. Harvest Festivals Around the World**

1. "The Four Species," Shamash: The Jewish Network, <http://listserv.shamash.org/cgi-bin/wa?A2=ind041005&L=top&T=0&P=64> (May 21, 2006).

2. Selena Fox, "Cornucopia: Horn of Plenty," *Circle Magazine*, Fall 2000, pp. 34–35, <http://www.circlesanctuary.org/circle/articles/ritualtools/cornucopia.html> (May 18, 2006).

3. "The Legend of Huminodun," *Borneo Legends*, June 2000, <http://www.eborneo.com/insideborneo/legend0007.html> (May 19, 2006).

4. "September 24th: The Feast of Ingathering," *Chambers' Book of Days*, n.d., <http://www.thebookofdays.com/months/sept/24.htm> (May 21, 2006).

5. Ibid.

6. Erin Jessop, "Green Corn Festival," *Celebrations: A Social Studies Guide for Elementary Teachers*, Fall 1996, <http://teacherlink.ed.usu.edu/tlresources/units/Byrnes-celebrations/corn.html> (May 24, 2006).

7. Ibid.

❖ Chapter 2. The Life of Maulana Karenga

1. "144 Hours in August," University of Southern California Digital Library,<http://www.usc. edu/libraries/archives/cityinstress/mccone/ party.html> (May 27, 2006).

2. J. Lawrence Scholer, "The Story of Kwanzaa," *Dartmouth Review*, January 15, 2001, <http://www.dartreview.com/archives/2001/ 01/15/the_story_of_kwanzaa.php> (May 29, 2006).

3. Marcus Reeves, reviewer, Scot Brown, author, *Fighting for Us: Maulana Karenga, the US Organization, and Black Cultural Nationalism*, San Francisco *Chronicle*, August 3, 2003, <http://www.mindfully.org/Reform/2003/ Karenga-Fighting-For-US3aug03.htm> (May 28, 2006).

4. Maulana Karenga, *The Quotable Karenga* (Los Angeles: US Organization, 1967), p. 5.

5. Quoted in Monica Moorehead, "Fred Hampton Day Declared," *Workers World*, December 16, 2004, <http://lists.econ.utah.edu/pipermail/ margins-to-centre/2005-April/000385.html> (June 16, 2006).

6. Scholer.

7. Quoted in Gerry Wachovsky, "Forty-Niner Does Not Need to Apologize to Convict," California State University at Long Beach, *Online 49er*, vol. LV, no. 112, <http://www.csulb.edu/~d49er/ archives/2005/spring/opinion/volLVno112- apologize.shtml> (May 31, 2006).

8. Gwendolyn E. Osborne, "It's Beginning to Look A Lot Like Kwanzaa," *Black Issues Book Review*, November 2000, <http://www.findarticles.

com/p/articles/mi_m0HST/is_6_2/ai_
67151369> (June 3, 2006).

◆ **Chapter 3. Kwanzaa and African-American Culture**

1. Mary Bellis, "Inventors: George Washington
    Carver," *About.com*, n.d., <http://inventors.
    about.com/library/weekly/aa041897.htm>
    (June 18, 2006).
2. Alex Haley, *Roots: The Saga of an American
    Family* (New York: Dell Publishing, 1976), p. 11.
3. Dr. Carolyn Holmes and Dianne Partee, "Meet
    the Griot," *Culture Connection*, October 2, 2001,
    School District of Philadelphia, <http://
    www.phila.k12.pa.us/offices/imedia/
    Meetthegriot.html> (July 14, 2006).
4. Booker T. Washington, *Up From Slavery: An
    Autobiography* (New York: Penguin Books,
    1986), pp. 34–35.
5. Robert Cameron Mitchell, Donald George
    Morrison, and John Naber Paden, *Black Africa:
    A Comparative Handbook, Second Edition* (New
    York: Paragon House, 1989), p. 25.
6. Gina Philogene, *From Black to African American:
    A New Social Representation* (Westport, Conn.:
    Praeger Publishers, 1999), p. iii.
7. Mary Pattillo-McCoy, *Black Picket Fences:
    Privilege and Peril Among the Black Middle Class*
    (Chicago: University of Chicago Press, 1999),
    p. 3.
8. Maulana Karenga, *The African American Holiday
    of Kwanzaa: A Celebration of Family, Community
    and Culture* (Los Angeles: University of Sankore
    Press, 1989), p. 11.

9. "Fundamental Questions About Kwanzaa: An Interview," *The Official Kwanzaa Web Site*, n.d., <http://www.officialkwanzaawebsite.org/faq.s html#5> (August 5, 2006).

10. "History of Juneteenth," *Juneteenth.com*, 1996–2005, <http://www.juneteenth.com/ history.htm> (July 25, 2006).

11. James W. Johnson, Ph.D., F. Frances Johnson, Ph.D., and Ronald L. Slaughter, Ph.D., *The Nguzo Saba and the Festival of First Fruits: A Guide for Promoting Family, Community Values and the Celebration of Kwanzaa* (New York: Gumbs & Thomas Publishers, 1995), p. 6.

12. "Kwanzaa in Canada," *Cool Women*, n.d., <http://www.coolwomen.ca/coolwomen/cwsite. nsf/vwWeek/A01C5730424A63DA852569BB00 1209C6?OpenDocument> (August 1, 2006).

13. "USVI Kwanzaa Celebration Begins," *Caribbean Net News*, December 29, 2005, <http://www. caribbeannetnews.com/2005/12/29/begins.sh tml> (August 1, 2006).

❖ Chapter 4. Symbols, Rituals, and Traditions

1. "Five Fundamental Activities of Kwanzaa," Natural History Museum of Los Angeles County Web site, n.d., <http://www.nhm.org/africa/ america/kwanzaa/five.htm> (February 20, 2007).

2. Dorothy Winbush Riley, *The Complete Kwanzaa: Celebrating Our Cultural Harvest* (New York: HarperCollins, 1995), pp.22–23.

3. "Kwanzaa: Rituals and Ceremony," National Rights of Passage Institute Web site, 2002, <http://

www.ritesofpassage.org/kwanzaaceremony. htm> (February 20, 2007).

4. Adapted from James W. Johnson, Ph.D., F. Frances Johnson, Ph.D., and Ronald L. Slaughter, Ph.D., *The Nguzo Saba and the Festival of First Fruits: A Guide for Promoting Family, Community Values and the Celebration of Kwanzaa* (New York: Gumbs & Thomas Publishers, 1995), pp. 81–82.

5. Lamine Konte. "The Griot: Singer and Chronicler of African Life," *UNESCO Courier*, April, 1986, <http://www.findarticles.com/p/articles/ mi_m1310/is_1986_April/ai_4190852/pg_1>

◈ Chapter 5. The Principles of Kwanzaa

1. Jessica B. Harris, *A Kwanzaa Keepsake: Celebrating the Holiday with New Traditions and Feasts* (New York: Simon & Schuster, 1995), p. 30.

2. Quoted in Maulana Karenga, *The African American Holiday of Kwanzaa: A Celebration of Family, Community and Culture* (Los Angeles: University of Sankore Press, 1989), p. 52.

3. Ibid., p. 70.

◈ Chapter 6. Celebrating Kwanzaa Today

1. "The African Pledge," *The Afrocentric Experience*, n.d., <http://www.swagga.com/pledge.htm> (August 4, 2006).

2. Gail Forsyth-Vail, "Lessons From the Kwanzaa Candles," Unitarian Sunday School Society, 1999, <http://www.uua.org/re/reach/worship/ kwanzaa.html> (September 30, 2006).

3. Yvonne V. Jones, "African-American Cultural Nationalism," *Cultural Portrayals of African Americans: Creating an Ethnic/Racial Identity,* Janis Faye Hutchinson, ed. (Westport, Conn.: Bergin & Garvey, 1997), p. 129.
4. Jessica B. Harris, *A Kwanzaa Keepsake: Celebrating the Holiday with New Traditions and Feasts* (New York: Simon & Schuster, 1995), p. 128.
5. Ibid., p. 132.

FURTHER READING

Cole, Harriette, and John Pinderhughes. *Coming Together: Celebrations for African American Families.* New York: Jump at the Sun, 2003.

Johnson, Dolores. *The Children's Book of Kwanzaa: A Guide to Celebrating the Holiday.* New York: Simon and Schuster, 1997.

Jones, Amy Robin. *Kwanzaa.* Chanhassen, Minn.: Child's World, 2001.

Kimble-Ellis, Sonya. *Traditional African American Arts and Activities.* New York: John Wiley & Sons, 2002.

Rau, Dana Meachen. *Kwanzaa.* New York: Children's Press, 2000.

Riley, D. Winbush. *The Complete Kwanzaa: Celebrating Our Cultural Harvest.* Castle Books, 2003.

INTERNET ADDRESSES

The Official Kwanzaa Web Site
  <http://www.officialkwanzaawebsite.org/index.
    shtml>
  Learn more about Kwanzaa from the official Web site.

Kwanzaa
  <http://www.kidsdomain.com/holiday/kwanzaa>
  Find crafts, games, and more at this Web site.

INDEX

A

African arts, 81
African-Americans
    other names for, 37,
        39
African Heritage, 34–35,
    37, 39, 49, 58
Afro-American Studies
    (UCLA), 26
agricultural revolution, 6
Ali, Muhammad, 35
Aninha, Mae, 69
Armstrong, Louis, 34

B

Bethune, Mary McLeod,
    69
Bibb, Mary, 48
Black Panthers, 26–28
Borneo, harvest myth of,
    13–14

C

California State
    University, 31
Canadian Kwanzaa, 48

candles
    activities with, 84–85
Caribbean Kwanzaa, 49
Carver, George
    Washington, 34
communal meals, 86
cultural nationalism, 25,
    27

D

Davis, Gail, 28

E

Edelman, Marian Wright,
    73
emancipation,, 35
English Kwanzaa, 48
Everett, Ronald, 19–21,
    23, 25

F

Festival of Booths. See
    Succoth
folklore, 9
Four Species, 8, 9, 11

G

Garvey, Marcus, 69

ghetto, 33, 42
Green Corn Festival, 16
griots, 36, 61–63, 82

H
habari gani, 60, 67
Hamer, Fannie Lou, 72
Harris, Jessica B., 67, 86
Harvest Home, 15–16
Horn of Plenty, 13

I
Islamic faith, 35

J
Jabbar, Kareem Abdul, 35
Jones, Deborah, 28
Joplin, Scott, 34
Jordan, Michael, 70

K
Kenyatta, Jomo, 70
King, Martin Luther, Jr., 20, 27, 67
Kinoingan, god of Borneo, 13

L
libation, 58, 59, 61, 67, 81
Lift Every Voice and Sing, 49

Los Angeles City College, 20

M
Malcolm X, 21–23, 35
Marshall, Thurgood, 73
matunda ya kwanza "first fruits", 51
middle class, African American, 39, 42
myth, 9, 13

N
names, changing, 22, 25, 35
National Association for the Advancement of Colored People (NAACP), 39
Nation of Islam, 22, 23
Nkrumah, Kwame, 69
non-blacks and Kwanzaa, 44

P
Powell, Colin, 70

R
racism, 19, 26, 33, 39
ritual, 8–9, 11, 14, 16, 17, 47, 52, 58, 60, 61, 67, 77, 81, 87

S
segregation, 20, 33, 73
Shaka Zulu, 70
slavery, freedom from,
    33, 34–35, 46
Smith, Bessie, 34
storytelling., 61
Succoth, 6, 8, 9, 11
Swahili language, 25, 51,
    60
symbol, 5, 8, 9, 11, 45,
    52, 53, 57, 58, 77

U
United States University,
    28

University of California
    at Los Angeles
    (UCLA), 25, 26
Us (organization), 25–26,
    28

W
Walking the Parachute,
    85–86
Watts riots, 23, 25

Z
Zeus (Greek god), 11, 13